A TRUE BOOK™

Alternative Energy
Wind Power

Sailboats, Windmills, and Wind Turbines

MATTHEW ZIEM

Children's Press®
An Imprint of Scholastic Inc.

Content Consultant
Kevin Doran, J.D., Institute Fellow and Research Professor,
Renewable and Sustainable Energy Institute,
University of Colorado at Boulder

Library of Congress Cataloging-in-Publication Data

Names: Ziem, Matthew, author.
Title: Wind power : sailboats, windmills, and wind turbines / by Matthew Ziem.
Other titles: True book.
Description: New York, NY : Children's Press, an imprint of Scholastic Inc.,
  [2018] | Series: A true book
Identifiers: LCCN 2018009072| ISBN 9780531236888 (library binding) | ISBN
  9780531239452 (pbk.)
Subjects: LCSH: Wind power--Juvenile literature. | Wind power
  plants--Juvenile literature.
Classification: LCC TJ820 .Z54 2018 | DDC 621.31/2136--dc23 LC record available at
https://lccn.loc.gov/2018009072

All rights reserved. Published in 2019 by Children's Press, an imprint of Scholastic Inc.
Printed in Heshan, China 62

Scholastic Inc., 557 Broadway, New York, NY 10012

3 4 5 6 7 8 9 10 R 28 27 26 25 24 23 22

Front cover: Wind turbine technician
Back cover: Windsurfer near a wind farm

Find the Truth!

Everything you are about to read is true *except* for one of the sentences on this page.

Which one is **TRUE**?

T or F By 2030, wind power could supply 20 percent of the nation's electricity.

T or F The strongest, most constant winds blow on land, near the ground.

Find the answers in this book.

Contents

THE BIG TRUTH!

Pros and Cons

Windsurfing

4

Flying wind turbine

4 The Future of Wind Power

What are the latest technologies
in wind energy?

Windmill

A Need for Alternative Energy

We use energy every day. It fuels cars and powers cell phones. It cools homes when it's hot outside and warms them when the weather turns cold. It provides light through the night while the sun shines on the other half of the world.

All this energy must come from somewhere. Since the 1700s, people have relied mostly on fossil fuels such as coal, oil, and natural gas. These materials burn easily to create heat and can be turned into electricity. But they are far from perfect.

Our supply of fossil fuels is limited. Experts predict that **fossil fuels will dwindle and their cost will rise**. In addition, **burning these fuels releases harmful substances**.

Some substances trap heat within the **atmosphere**, leading to **climate change**. Others cause health problems, including heart and lung diseases.

What Can We Do?

Renewable energy sources such as **solar**, water, geothermal, and wind are healthier sources than fossil fuels. They can serve our electricity needs while reducing the damage done to the planet and us.

Turn the page to learn how we can use the natural movement of air to generate electricity. Learn the secrets of wind power!

Kites were invented more than 2,000 years ago in ancient China.

CHAPTER 1

An Invisible Power

Even though wind is invisible, we can see it in action just about everywhere we look. Birds soar on it. It sends autumn leaves skittering across lawns and kites flying through the air. It carries plant seeds from place to place. It sculpts desert dunes and makes flags flap atop their poles. We also move the air when we whistle, blow up a balloon, or wave a hand fan back and forth.

Short gusts of wind can exceed 200 miles (322 kilometers) per hour in hurricanes.

Energy in the Air

The air outside is rarely still. Sometimes there might be raging winds from storms. Other times there might be only the faintest breeze. But even if the air feels almost completely still, it is blowing harder somewhere else on Earth. This is what makes wind such a great source of energy. It is always around us, and it is always moving. It is also completely renewable. This means there will always be more wind, no matter how much people use.

What Is Wind?

Wind is simply moving air. What makes it move? The main cause is the sun's uneven heating of the earth. Air is warmer in some places than in others. When air warms, it expands, becoming less dense. This makes it rise. When it cools it condenses, becoming more dense. This makes it sink. Why? Imagine marshmallows floating in cocoa. The airy marshmallows are less dense than the cocoa. As a result, they float. Air behaves the same way. Warm air floats above the denser cool air.

A leaf's wide, flat shape makes it easy to catch the wind.

Under Pressure

So why does wind blow from side to side instead of up and down? The answer has to do with **air pressure**. When warm air rises, it leaves behind an area of low air pressure. The gases in our air always move from high pressure areas toward low pressure areas. So as warm air rises, cooler air rushes in to take its place. We experience this air movement as wind, whether it's a pleasant breeze or a blustery storm.

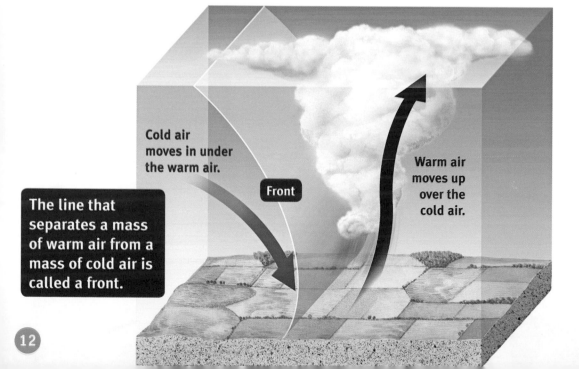

Cold air moves in under the warm air.

Front

Warm air moves up over the cold air.

The line that separates a mass of warm air from a mass of cold air is called a front.

The strongest tornado winds ever recorded reached 318 miles (512 km) per hour.

In certain conditions, winds can form into a funnel called a tornado.

On the Move

Kinetic energy is the energy of motion. When you throw a ball, that ball has kinetic energy. The air is no different. When it moves, it has kinetic energy. People capture this energy all the time. Wind keeps kites and gliders aloft on a windy day. It fills a boat's sails, pushing the craft along the water. This energy can also power **turbines**. They work like pinwheels to capture the wind's energy. Then they turn this energy into usable electricity.

Invented in the 1960s, the sport of windsurfing combines sailing and surfing.

CHAPTER 2

Blowing Through History

Thousands of years ago, wind was one of the only energy sources available. Wind made it possible for people to travel, process foods, and even make music. Over time, human innovations and technology advancements made these wind-related processes more **efficient** and effective.

Ancient Egyptians used sails to power their boats and large paddles to help steer.

Riding the Waves

The earliest use of wind energy was for sailing. People have been sailing for thousands of years. The ancient Sumerians of Mesopotamia lived in what is now southern Iraq. They sailed the great Tigris and Euphrates Rivers. The ancient Egyptians navigated the Nile River in sailboats. These and other early peoples relied on sailboats to fish, transport goods, and wage war. Later, wind power helped brave adventurers sail the seas and explore the world.

A sail is little more than a piece of cloth held upright by a system of poles and ropes. It's attached to a boat. The sail catches the wind, capturing its kinetic energy. This energy is then transferred to the vehicle, pushing it forward along the top of the water or other surface.

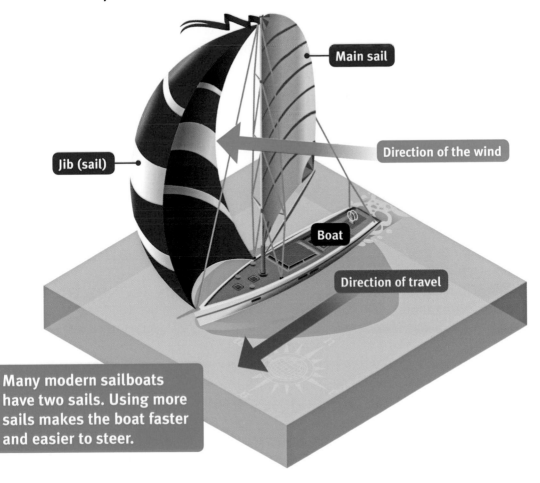

Main sail

Jib (sail)

Direction of the wind

Boat

Direction of travel

Many modern sailboats have two sails. Using more sails makes the boat faster and easier to steer.

Sailors use ropes and pulleys to adjust the positions of sails.

A sailboat does not need to travel in the exact same direction as the wind. A sailor can control the direction of a boat by changing the angle of the sail. Changing the angle of a sail changes the air pressure around it. This makes the wind around the sail move in the direction a sailor wants it to. No matter where the wind comes from, a vehicle with a sail can move in any direction.

Wind Music

Did you know that the wind can make music? Every time a gentle breeze rustles a wind chime, you are hearing a kind of wind music. But there is also a musical instrument that is actually played by the wind. It's called an aeolian harp. The aeolian harp is named for Aeolus, the ancient Greek god of wind. When the wind blows across the harp's strings, they vibrate and produce a pleasant yet haunting sound. The sound changes based on the speed and direction of the wind.

Outside the Exploratorium in San Francisco, California, a huge aeolian harp stands 27 feet (8.2 m) tall.

19

These windmills stood near Alexandria, Egypt, in the 1800s.

Spinning in the Wind

Windmills have also been around for thousands of years. A windmill captures the wind's energy and uses it to power machinery. No one knows for sure when the first one was invented. However, experts know windmills were used in ancient Persia (modern Iran) by at least the 800s CE. Windmills soon spread through the Middle East and Asia. They appeared in Europe by the 1100s, and European settlers brought them to America in the 1600s.

Most traditional windmills use four or more sails called vanes to catch the wind. Vanes are made from cloth stretched across a wooden frame. Other windmills use rigid blades made from wood or metal. When the wind hits a windmill's vanes or blades, it causes them to rotate. This motion turns a wooden shaft. As the shaft rotates, it causes a series of gears inside the windmill to turn.

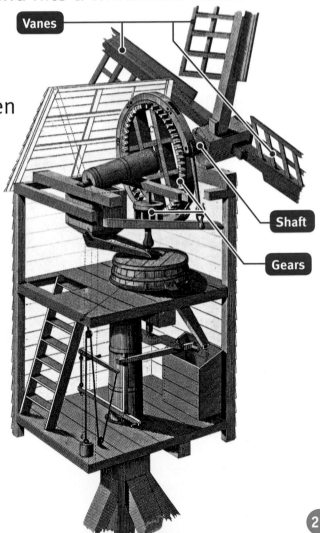

Vanes

Shaft

Gears

This European windmill from the 1800s works much the same as a modern windmill.

The gears inside the windmill can operate a variety of machines. Early windmills were most often used to grind grain into flour. This process can be long and difficult if done by hand. But windmills made it fast and easy. Windmills were also built near water. As the wind turned the windmill's vanes, the machine inside would pump water. People used windmills to drain flooded land or get water out of deep wells.

The Netherlands has many windmills that, along with other machines, pump water out of areas that are prone to flooding.

It's Electric!

In 1887, Scottish scientist James Blyth discovered that windmills could do more than grind grain and pump water. He realized they could also create electricity by turning the gears of electrical **generators**. Soon after Blyth's discoveries, others around the world began building on them. A new era in wind energy was starting.

At first, no one was interested in the electricity Blyth produced with his wind turbine.

The people who fix and maintain turbines are called wind turbine technicians, or "windtechs" for short.

A worker stands atop a turbine at a wind farm in California.

CHAPTER 3

From Wind to Electricity

Energy is constant. There is always the same amount in the universe. It cannot be created or destroyed. It can only be turned from one kind of energy into another. Today, wind energy is mostly used to create electricity. To do this, the energy in the wind must be transformed, or changed. Power plants that rely on wind have special equipment to transform the wind that rustles leaves into the electricity that runs our homes.

What Is a Wind Turbine?

A turbine is any machine that uses the energy of moving liquid or gas to spin a shaft that performs some kind of work. In this sense, early windmills were turbines. But today, the term *wind turbine* generally refers to a machine that turns wind energy into electricity. Wind turbines are the opposite of fans. Electricity turns a fan's blades to create wind. But with a turbine, wind turns the turbine to create electricity.

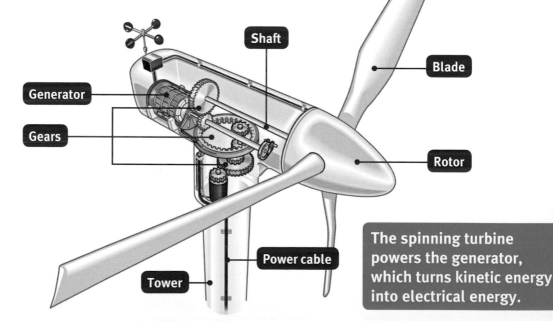

Shaft

Blade

Generator

Gears

Rotor

Power cable

Tower

The spinning turbine powers the generator, which turns kinetic energy into electrical energy.

Modern wind turbine

Traditional windmill

Both modern turbines and traditional windmills are a common sight in The Netherlands today.

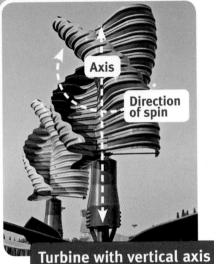

Axis

Direction of spin

Turbine with vertical axis

Big and Small

Early windmills were often about as tall as a three-story house. But modern wind turbines can be much bigger—and much smaller. Some tower more than 600 feet (183 meters) high. And each turbine blade can be more than 240 feet (73 m) long! Some of the tallest are in Europe. The smallest turbines are portable. Campers, mountain climbers, and scientists can carry them to power equipment in the wilderness. Some turbines also have unique shapes. For example, many new ones have a vertical, or up-and-down, axis.

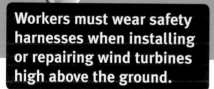

Looking for a Location

Wind turbines must be placed where there is plenty of wind. Otherwise, they won't work correctly. To make electricity, large wind turbines need winds that regularly blow at a minimum of 6 miles (9.7 km) per hour. Good locations include hills, open fields, and wide plains. Many are placed offshore, away from land. Wind turbines need to be far away from buildings or trees that could block the wind. But they can't be too far from the power stations they supply with electricity.

Workers must wear safety harnesses when installing or repairing wind turbines high above the ground.

Farming the Wind

Look at this photo. It is a wind farm. It is an area where many turbines are grouped together. The first one was built in New Hampshire in 1980. It contained 20 wind turbines. China is home to the biggest collection of wind farms in the world. The largest wind farms have thousands of turbines across hundreds of square miles. Each turbine needs to be spaced out from the others. If they are too close together, they will get in each other's way.

A large wind farm can cover huge areas of open space.

Wind Above the Water

Offshore winds are usually stronger and steadier. As a result, offshore wind farms generate more electricity than ones on land. The turbines in these watery wind farms are among the largest in the world. Because they are anchored to the seafloor, most offshore turbines are built in shallow waters near land.

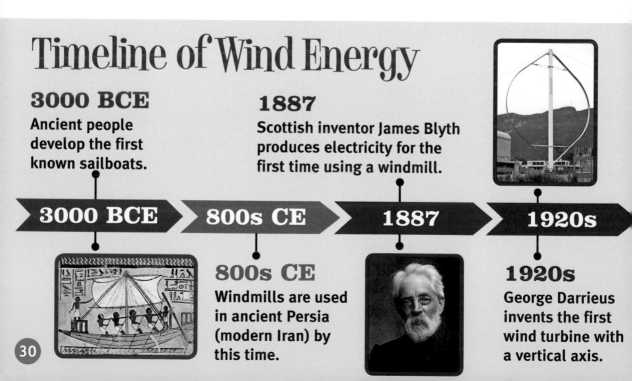

Timeline of Wind Energy

3000 BCE
Ancient people develop the first known sailboats.

1887
Scottish inventor James Blyth produces electricity for the first time using a windmill.

| 3000 BCE | 800s CE | 1887 | 1920s |

800s CE
Windmills are used in ancient Persia (modern Iran) by this time.

1920s
George Darrieus invents the first wind turbine with a vertical axis.

Charging Up

The electricity generated by wind farms is usually sent to the public electrical grid. The grid distributes the electricity to homes and businesses. Electricity generated by wind turbines can also be stored in batteries. This allows turbines to supply power even when the wind isn't blowing strong. Because wind can be unpredictable, storing electricity in batteries can make wind energy more effective.

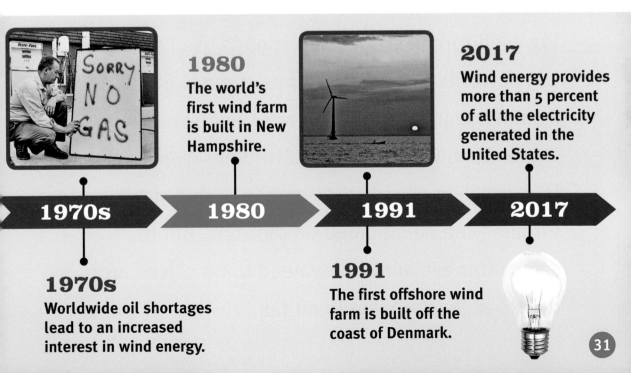

1980
The world's first wind farm is built in New Hampshire.

2017
Wind energy provides more than 5 percent of all the electricity generated in the United States.

1970s — **1980** — **1991** — **2017**

1970s
Worldwide oil shortages lead to an increased interest in wind energy.

1991
The first offshore wind farm is built off the coast of Denmark.

Wind Energy at Home

Big wind turbines, such as the ones used offshore, can power thousands of homes at once! But what if someone just wants to power their own home? There are many smaller wind turbines available for supplying electricity to homes. These small turbines can be mounted on rooftops. But to catch stronger winds, they need to be placed atop towers at least 30 feet (9 m) tall.

Not every home is a good fit for wind power. To make sure there is enough wind available to use wind power, a home needs at least 1 acre (0.4 hectare) of open space around it. This means homes in dense cities are not well suited for installing wind turbines. However, wind turbines are a great source of energy for buildings located in remote areas where other power sources might not be available.

Wind turbines may be attached to the top of a house to catch winds.

Pros and Cons

Wind is powerful. It is cleaner and more sustainable than other energy sources. But is it the perfect replacement for fuels such as coal or oil? You decide.

Coal mine

The **PROS** about Wind Energy

1. It is available everywhere. Fossil fuels can only be found in certain places.
2. It does not release any harmful gases into the atmosphere. In contrast, the gases released by burning fossil fuels are a cause of climate change.
3. It is renewable, while Earth only has a limited supply of fossil fuels.
4. In the long run, it is cheaper than fossil fuels.

Pollution from processing oil

Cheaper in the long run

Bat

Wind farm

The CONS
about Wind Energy

1 Wind energy is **variable**. We cannot predict its strength and direction. It doesn't always blow strong enough to power a generator.

2 Wind farms take up a lot of space, and most wind turbines are very large.

3 Some people think wind farms are ugly and ruin the appearance of natural landscapes.

4 Turbines can kill or injure birds and bats.

5 Getting started with wind energy is expensive. Installing a wind turbine for a single home can cost as much as $70,000!

6 Turbines can be loud, affecting those who live nearby.

Expensive to get started

A flying turbine like this one in Alaska can float up to 1,000 feet (305 m) above the ground.

CHAPTER 4

The Future of Wind Power

Residents in Fairbanks, Alaska, woke up one morning in 2015 and saw giant balloons floating high in the sky. It wasn't a parade! It was an experiment with flying turbines. Each turbine had a shell that inflated and made it float into the sky. Researchers hope that in the near future this kind of turbine will bring power to remote areas around the world.

Powering the Future

Wind power companies are always experimenting with new turbine designs like the ones tested in Alaska. High in the sky where these turbines would fly, winds are stronger. This is why they would be able to create more electricity. The turbines would not require the land needed by current wind farms. Inventors are also testing turbines without any blades. Wind makes these poles sway. This movement is turned into electricity. Such turbines would be safer and cheaper than today's turbines, while taking up less space.

Protecting Birds

Experts believe that between 140,000 and 328,000 birds die each year from being hit by turbine blades. Scientists in wind power companies are working to prevent these deaths. They have come up with different methods. One way involves using camera systems to detect approaching birds so turbines can be shut down in time. Another involves using turbines with slower-moving blades that are easier for birds to avoid. Turbines without any blades at all will also solve this problem.

A crane is used to lift a massive rotor onto a wind turbine.

A Piece of the Energy Pie

Wind power generates more electricity in the United States than any other renewable energy source. Currently, more than 5 percent of all the electricity used in the United States comes from wind. This is enough to power more than 25 million homes! By 2030, wind power could supply 20 percent of the nation's electricity.

However, wind power will probably never supply all of the world's energy needs. But together with other kinds of **alternative** energy, such as solar power and water power, it can play an important role in reducing the pollution caused by burning harmful fossil fuels.

By using clean, renewable energy sources such as wind, we can make our world a greener and healthier place for all living things! ★

The experimental Sky Serpent wind turbine attaches several rotors together. Here, a balloon holds up one end of the line of rotors.

Looking Back at the Book

What have you learned? Here's a quick review!
Can you add any details to the bits and pieces below?

PAGE 10

Benefits of using wind energy

★ It is everywhere.
★ It is renewable.

PAGES 11–12

What causes wind to blow?

The sun warms the air around the planet unevenly.

Warm air rises.

Cooler air moves in to fill the space left behind by the rising warm air.

PAGES 15–22

Early wind power technology

Sailboats

Windmills

PAGES
15-23

Uses of wind energy

★ **Powering vehicles that move on water**

★ **Pumping water**

★ **Grinding grain into flour**

★ **Generating electricity**

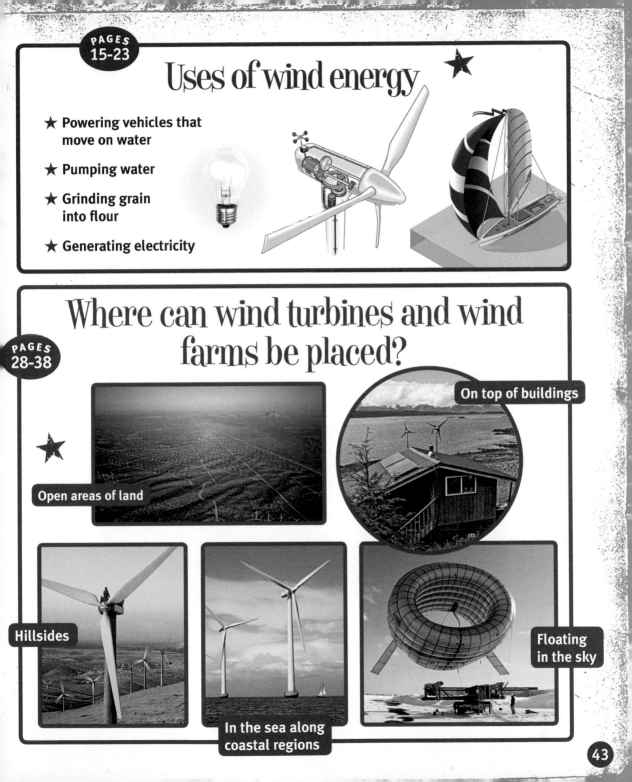

PAGES
28-38

Where can wind turbines and wind farms be placed?

On top of buildings

Open areas of land

Hillsides

In the sea along coastal regions

Floating in the sky

True Statistics

Maximum speed of a ship under sail power: About 75 mi. (121 km) per hour

Height of today's tallest wind turbines: Turbines in Germany reach as high as 809 ft. (247 m)

Highest wind speed ever recorded: 254 mi. 409 km) per hour, in Australia

Blade speed of modern wind turbine: More than 200 mi. (322 km) per hour

Average length of wind turbine blade: More than 160 ft. (49 m)

Number of blades on a modern wind turbine: Usually 3

Nation that produces the most wind energy per year: China

Did you find the truth?

By 2030, wind power could supply 20 percent of the nation's electricity.

The strongest, most constant winds blow on land, near the ground.

Resources

Books

Allen, Kathy. *Wind Power*. Ann Arbor, MI: Cherry Lake Publishing, 2013.

Benduhn, Tea. *Wind Power*. Pleasantville, NY: Weekly Reader, 2009.

Mara, Wil. *Wind Turbine Services Technician*. Ann Arbor, MI: Cherry Lake Publishing, 2013.

Muschal, Frank. *Energy From Wind, Sun, and Tides*. Ann Arbor, MI: Cherry Lake Publishing, 2008.

Otfinoski, Steven. *Wind, Solar, and Geothermal Power: From Concept to Consumer*. New York: Children's Press, 2016.

Pettiford, Rebecca. *Wind Power*. Minneapolis: Pogo, 2017.

Visit this Scholastic website for more information on Wind Power:
⭐ www.factsfornow.scholastic.com
Enter the keywords **Wind Power**

Important Words

air pressure (AIR PRESH-ur) a measurement of the force produced by air on the things it surrounds

alternative (awl-TUR-nuh-tiv) a choice that is not the usual one

atmosphere (AT-muhs-feer) the mixture of gases that surrounds a planet

climate change (KLYE-mit CHAYNJ) global warming and other changes in the weather and weather patterns that are happening because of human activity

efficient (ih-FISH-uhnt) working very well and not wasting time or energy

generators (JEN-uh-ray-turz) machines that produce electricity by turning a magnet inside a coil of wire

solar (SOH-lur) of or having to do with the sun

turbines (TUR-buhnz) engines powered by water, steam, wind, or gas passing through the blades of a wheel and making it spin

variable (VAIR-ee-uh-buhl) likely to change

Index

Page numbers in **bold** indicate illustrations.

About the Author

Matthew Ziem has a bachelor's degree in English from Marist College. He has been an editor of children's reference products for more than 20 years. In this role, he has learned about many topics, but especially about animals and nature. This is his first book. Matt lives in New Fairfield, Connecticut, where he is always on the lookout for ways to help wildlife and the environment.